More Piggyback Songs for School

Written and Compiled by the Totline Staff

Illustrated by Marion Hopping Ekberg

Chorded by Barbara Robinson

Warren Publishing House
Everett, WA

Our special thanks go to Laura Egge of Oswego, Oregon, for her contributions to this book. We feel sure that her many wonderful songs, which appear throughout, will help you capture your children's attention and create the kind of atmosphere that allows learning to flourish.

Editorial Staff:
    Managing Editor: Kathleen Cubley
    Editors: Gayle Bittinger, Kate Ffolliott, Susan Hodges, Elizabeth McKinnon, Jean Warren
    Copy Editor: Kris Fulsaas
    Proofreader: Mae Rhodes

Design and Production Staff:
    Art Managers: Uma Kukathas, Jill Lustig
    Book Design/Layout Production: Sarah Ness
    Cover Design: Brenda Mann Harrison
    Cover Illustration: Marion Hopping Ekberg
    Production Manager: Jo Anna Brock

Copyright © 1995 by WARREN PUBLISHING HOUSE. All rights reserved. Except for the inclusion of brief quotations in a review, no part of this book may be reproduced or utilized in any form or by any means, electronic or mechanical, including photocopying, recording, or by any information storage and retrieval system, without written permission from the publisher.

Piggyback® is a registered trademark of Warren Publishing House.

ISBN 1-57029-067-9

Library of Congress Catalog Number 95-60006
Printed in the United States of America.
Published by: Warren Publishing House
              P.O. Box 2250
              Everett, WA 98203

20 19 18 17 16 15 14 13 12 11 10 9 8 7 6 5 4 3 2 1

Contents

Time for School
All About School 6
Getting Acquainted 8
Beginning of the Day 10
Songs to Sign 12
Guidance 14
Transition Times 16
Group Time 18
Language Time 20
Music Time 22
Snacktime 24
Naptime 27
Movement Time 29
Outdoor Time 32
Cleanup Time 34
End of the Day 37

Concepts
Colors 60
Shapes 63
Numbers 66
Letters 68
Opposites 69
Time 72
Calendar 73
Weather 75
Seasons 77
Multiple Concepts 79

Learning and Caring About Ourselves and Others
Safety 40
Health 43
Body Parts 46
Self-Esteem 48
Feelings 52
Sharing and Caring 53
Friends 56

Time for School

A Special Place
Sung to: *Twinkle, Twinkle, Little Star*

   C   F   C
Letters, numbers, shapes, and rules,
G₇   C   G₇   C
These are things we learn at school.
C   G₇   C   G₇
How to share and how to play,
C   G₇   C   G₇
How to have fun every day.
C   F   C
Going to school is so much fun,
  G₇   C   G₇   C
A special place for everyone.

Margery A. Kranyik
Hyde Park, MA

All in a Day at School
Sung to: *The Wheels on the Bus*

        C
The children at the school

Come to work and play,
  (Skip in a circle.)
G₇   C
Work and play, work and play.

The children at the school

Come to work and play,
G₇   C
Every day at school.

Continue with similar verses such as these: The doors at the school go open and shut; The children at the school like to build with blocks; The swings at the school go back and forth.

Jan Miller
Gatesville, TX

At School
Sung to: *Jimmy Crack Corn*

F   C₇
Coming to school every day,
             F
Coming to school every day,
             B♭
Coming to school every day
C₇   F
Helps us as we grow.

F   C₇
Playing at school every day,
            F
Playing at school every day,
            B♭
Playing at school every day
C₇   F
Helps us as we grow.

Additional verses: Learning at school every day; Sharing at school every day.

Margery A. Kranyik
Hyde Park, MA

School
Sung to: *Twinkle, Twinkle, Little Star*

C   F   C
School will teach me how to share,
G₇   C   G₇   C
How to tell a friend I care.
C   G₇   C   G₇
School will help me spell my name,
C   G₇   C   G₇
Help me learn to play a game.
C   F   C
School is where I like to be,
G₇   C   G₇   C
With my teachers helping me.

Margery A. Kranyik
Hyde Park, MA

Our Teachers Show the Way
Sung to: *The Farmer in the Dell*

      D
At school we laugh and play.

It's fun to learn all day,

Create, explore, and so much more!
A₇   D
Our teachers show the way.

Shannon Shorey
Orlando, FL

Who's at School?
Sung to: *Old MacDonald Had a Farm*

   F   B♭   F
Mrs. Williams has a class.
  C₇ F
E-I-E-I-O.
                     B♭   F
And in her class she has some children.
  C₇ F
E-I-E-I-O.

With Kevin here and Rachel there,

Here Daniel, there Katie,

Over here Nick and Tia.
               B♭   F
Mrs. Williams has a class.
  C₇ F
E-I-E-I-O.

Substitute your name for *Mrs. Williams* and the names of your children for those in the song. Continue singing until all your children have been named.

Laura Egge
Lake Oswego, OR

I'm Very Glad to Meet You
Sung to: *Skip to My Lou*

F
I am Teddy. What is your name?
  (First child gives name.)
C₇
I am Teddy. What is your name?
  (Next child gives name.)
F
I am Teddy. What is your name?
  (Next child gives name.)
C₇   F
I'm very glad to meet you.

Using a teddy bear as a puppet, continue singing the song until each child has had a turn.

Laura Egge
Lake Oswego, OR

8 Getting Acquainted

Who Are You?
Sung to: *The Mulberry Bush*

D
Tell me, tell me, tell me, do.
A₇
Tell me, do, who are you?
D
Let's roll the ball and find out who.
  (Roll a ball to one child.)
A₇   D
What, oh, what is your name?
  (Child says name.)

Sit on the floor in a circle and sing the song for each of your children.

Lisa Feeney
Pawling, NY

Getting Acquainted
Sung to: *Frere Jacques*

C
Who is hiding, who is hiding?

Who are you, who are you?

We think it is Libby.

We think it is Libby.

Is that true, is that true?

Have each child in turn cover his or her face. Then sing the song for the child, substituting his or her name for *Libby*.

Linda Filemyr
Baltimore, MD

It's Fun to Get to Know You
Sung to: *Did You Ever See a Lassie?*

         F
It's fun to get to know you,
      C₇   F
To know you, to know you.

It's fun to get to know you
    C₇   F
And be your friend
    C₇   F
To play with, to work with,
    C₇   F
To have so much fun with.

It's fun to get to know you
    C₇   F
And be your friend.

Patricia Coyne
Mansfield, MA

Getting Acquainted

Coming to School
Sung to: *The Mulberry Bush*

D
This is the way we come to school,
A₇
Come to school, come to school.
D
This is the way we come to school,
A₇   D
Early in the morning.

D
Some of us like to walk to school,
A₇
Walk to school, walk to school.
D
Some of us like to walk to school,
A₇   D
Early in the morning.

D
Some of us take the bus to school,
A₇
Bus to school, bus to school.
D
Some of us take the bus to school,
A₇   D
Early in the morning.

D
Some of us ride in the family car,
A₇
Family car, family car.
D
Some of us ride in the family car,
A₇   D
Early in the morning.

Continue with similar verses about ways your children come to school.

Margery A. Kranyik
Hyde Park, MA

H-e-l-l-o
Sung to: *Bingo*

F   B♭   F
When you greet someone you know,
         C   F
Hello is what you say-o.
     B♭   C   F   B♭
H-e-l-l-o, H-e-l-l-o, H-e-l-l-o.
C   F
Hello is what you say-o.

Janice Bodenstedt
Jackson, MI

Welcome to Our Group
Sung to: *Row, Row, Row Your Boat*

C
Welcome to our group.

We're glad you're here today.

We know you'll have a lot of fun
G   C
While you learn and play!

Kathy McCullough
St. Charles, IL

10 Beginning of the Day

Welcome, Friends
Sung to: *Goodnight, Ladies*

F
Welcome, new friends.
       C
Welcome, old friends.
F   Bb
Welcome, welcome.
      F   C   F
We're glad to see you all!
F
You are special.
  C
I am special.
F   Bb
We are so glad
     F   C   F
That we have such good pals!

Diane Thom
Maple Valley, WA

Welcome Song
Sung to: *Mary Had a Little Lamb*

C
Cody came to school today,
G₇   C
School today, school today.

Cody came to school today.
G₇   C
We're so glad he's here.

C
Let's all clap for Cody now,
   (Clap.)
G₇   C
Cody now, Cody now.

Let's all clap for Cody now
G₇   C
And give a great big cheer.
  (Give a cheer.)

Elizabeth McKinnon

Hurray, Hurray
Sung to: *Twinkle, Twinkle, Little Star*

C   F   C
Carmen's here. Hurray, hurray!
 G₇   C   G₇   C
I wonder what she'll do today.
C   G₇   C   G₇
Paint a picture? Play with toys?
C   G₇   C   G₇
Sing with other girls and boys?
C   F   G₇
Carmen's here. Hurray, hurray!
 G₇   C   G₇   C
I wonder what she'll do today.

Sing the song for each of your children, substituting the child's name for *Carmen* and something that the child might like to do for *paint a picture*.

Laura Egge
Lake Oswego, OR

Beginning of the Day

At Our School

Teach your children the following sign language phrase,
and then have fun as you sing and sign together the songs on page 13.

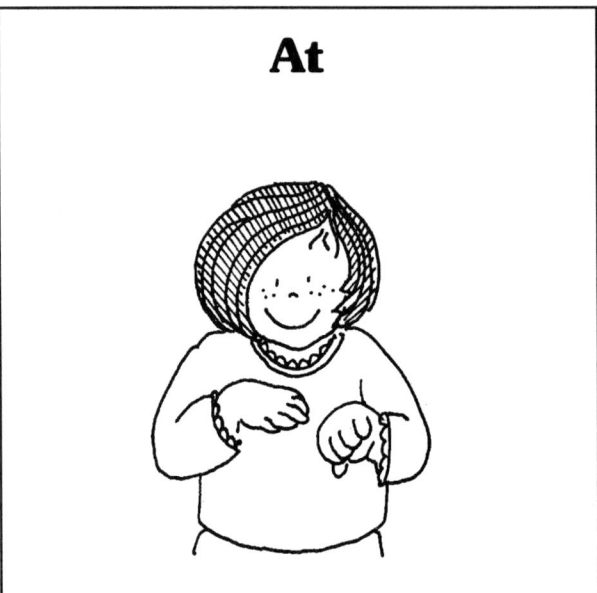

At

Touch fingertips of right hand to back of left hand.

Our

Place cupped right hand on right side of chest with thumb touching chest. Move hand in arc to left side of chest, ending with little finger touching chest.

School

Hold left hand palm up with fingers pointing right. Clap right hand, with palm down and fingers pointing left, twice on left hand.

12 Songs to Sign

Shh! It's Too Noisy
Sung to: *Pop! Goes the Weasel*

D   A₇   D
All around our room today,
       A₇   D
The children were so noisy.
       A₇   D
They couldn't hear the teacher say,
G A₇ D
"Shh! It's too noisy!"

*Laura Egge
Lake Oswego, OR*

Walking Feet
Sung to: *Frere Jacques*

C
Walking feet, walking feet.

See them slide, see them glide.

They never run inside the room,

They never run inside the room,

Just outside, just outside.

*Laura Egge
Lake Oswego, OR*

We Have Rules
Sung to: *Three Blind Mice*

C G₇ C G₇ C
We have rules, we have rules
  G₇ C G₇ C
In our school, in our school.
      G₇   C
We use inside voices and walking feet.
      G₇   C
We don't touch or bother the friends we meet.
    G₇   C
And when we're eating, we stay in our seats,
    G₇ C
'Cause we have rules.

*Priscilla M. Starrett
Warren, PA*

Getting Attention
Sung to: *If You're Happy and You Know It*

    F   C
If you can hear my voice, touch your nose.
    C   F
If you can hear my voice, touch your nose.
 B♭
If you're not making noise,
     F
You can surely hear my voice.
    C   F
If you can hear my voice, touch your nose.

Repeat, each time substituting a different phrase, such as *raise your hand* or *tap your toe,* for *touch your nose.*

Laura Egge
Lake Oswego, OR

Listen, Everyone
Sung to: *Twinkle, Twinkle, Little Star*

C   F   C
Listen, listen, everyone.
G₇   C G₇   C
Now our playing time is done.
C   G₇   C   G₇
Let's sit down, and let's be quiet.
C   G₇   C   G₇
We can do it if we try it.
C   F   C
Listen, listen, everyone.
G₇   C G₇   C
Now our playing time is done.

Substitute an appropriate time, such as *outdoor time* or *painting time,* for *playing time.*

Laura Egge
Lake Oswego, OR

Who Wants To?
Sung to: *London Bridge*

C
Who wants to do some painting now,
G₇   C
Painting now, painting now?

Who wants to do some painting now?
G₇   C
Who is ready?

Substitute an appropriate phrase, such as *do some cooking now* or *play a game with me,* for *do some painting now.*

Laura Egge
Lake Oswego, OR

Walk, Walk
Sung to: *Skip to My Lou*

F
Walk, walk, walk your feet.
C₇
Walk, walk, walk your feet.
F
Walk, walk, walk your feet.
C₇   F
Walk right to the sandbox.

Substitute the name of an appropriate destination, such as *snack table* or *playground,* for *sandbox.*

Gayle Bittinger

If You're Wearing Something Red
Sung to: *If You're Happy and You Know It*

      F   C
If you're wearing something red, get your coat.
      C   F
If you're wearing something red, get your coat.
      B♭
If you're wearing something red,
      F
If you're wearing something red,
      C   F
If you're wearing something red, get your coat.

Repeat, each time substituting the name of a different color for *red* or an appropriate phrase, such as *you may go* or *please wash up,* for *get your coat.*

Laura Egge
Lake Oswego, OR

Now It's Time
Sung to: *The Mulberry Bush*

D
Now it's time to go outside,
A₇
Go outside, go outside.
D
Now it's time to go outside,
  A₇   D
So early in the morning.

Substitute an appropriate phrase, such as *sit on the rug, eat our snack,* or *stand in line,* for *go outside.*

Laura Egge
Lake Oswego, OR

Who May Go?
Sung to: *London Bridge*

C
If you wore a hat today,
G₇   C
Hat today, hat today,

If you wore a hat today,
G₇   C
You may go now.

Repeat, each time substituting the name of a different article of clothing for *hat.*

Laura Egge
Lake Oswego, OR

Who Wants to Go?
Sung to: *Jimmy Crack Corn*

F   C₇
Who wants to go and play outside?
   (Adult sings.)

                          F
We want to go and play outside!
   (Everyone sings.)

                          B♭
Who wants to go and play outside?
   (Adult sings.)

C₇   F
We all want to go!
   (Everyone sings.)

Substitute an appropriate phrase, such as *go and stand in line* or *go to the library,* for *go and play outside.*

Laura Egge
Lake Oswego, OR

Come Around
Sung to: *Twinkle, Twinkle, Little Star*

C   F   C
Joseph and Kelsey, come around.
G₇   C   G₇   C
Peter and Ali, sit on the ground.
C   G₇   C   G₇
Abby and Tommy will sit next to you.
C   G₇   C   G₇
Emi, Billy, and Kim will, too.
C   F   C
Andrew, Andrew is the last one.
G₇   C   G₇   C
Now we're ready to have some fun!

Substitute the names of your children for those in the song.

Krista Alworth
Verona, NJ

We All Need to Sit Down
Sung to: *Frere Jacques*

C
Sit on the rug, sit on the rug
   (Sit on rug.)

Like we should, like we should.

We all need to sit down,

We all need to sit down.

Very good. Very good.

Substitute an appropriate word, such as *floor* or *chairs,* for *rug.*

Laura Egge
Lake Oswego, OR

Ready to Listen
Sung to: *Twinkle, Twinkle, Little Star*

C   F   C
Let your hands go clap, clap, clap.
   (Clap hands.)
G₇   C   G₇   C
Let your fingers go snap, snap, snap.
   (Snap fingers.)
C   G₇   C   G₇
Let your lips go up and down,
   (Open and close mouth.)
C   G₇   C   G₇
But don't let them make a sound.
   (Hold finger to lips.)
C   F   C
Fold your hands and close each eye.
   (Fold hands and close eyes.)
G₇   C   G₇   C
Take a breath, then softly sigh.
   (Breath deeply and say, "Ahhh.")

Adapted Traditional

I Am Talking
Sung to: *Frere Jacques*

C
I am talking, I am talking.

Quiet, please. Quiet, please.

It's my turn to talk now.

It's my turn to talk now.

Listen, please. Listen, please.

Laura Egge
Lake Oswego, OR

Circle Time
Sung to: *Twinkle, Twinkle, Little Star*

C   F   C
Here's my ribbon, flat as can be.
    G_7 C G_7 C
I'm going to give it some wiggles, you see.
     (Hold up piece of ribbon.)
C   F   C G_7
Watch me wiggle it, oh, so high.
C   F   C G_7
Watch me toss it up in the sky.
     (Wiggle ribbon and toss it away.)
C   F   C
All my wiggles are gone from me.
  G_7 C G_7 C
I gave them to my ribbon, as you can see.
     (Sit quietly with hands folded.)

Give each of your children a piece of ribbon before singing the song.

Patty Claycomb
Ventura, CA

Hush, Little Children
Sung to: *Hush, Little Baby*

F
Hush, little children,
C_7
Listen to me.

You'll like this story,
F
Just wait and see.
                  C_7
And if you're very quiet,

My friends,

You'll have a turn to talk
          F
When the story ends.

Laura Egge
Lake Oswego, OR

If a Wiggle's in Your Leg
Sung to: *If You're Happy and You Know It*

   F   C
If a wiggle's in your leg, shake it out.
    (Shake leg.)
   C   F
If a wiggle's in your leg, shake it out.
     B♭
If you have a little wiggle,
     F
It will surely make you giggle.
   C   F
If a wiggle's in your leg, shake it out.

Repeat, each time substituting the name of a different body part for *leg*.

Laura Egge
Lake Oswego, OR

A Story
Sung to: *Mary Had a Little Lamb*

C
Would you like to hear a story,
G₇   C
Hear a story, hear a story?

Would you like to hear a story?
G₇   C
If so, sit with me.

Angela Metzendorf
Kinsman, OH

Take a Look
Sung to: *If You're Happy and You Know It*

    F   C
Take a look, take a look at my book.
    C   F
Take a look, take a look at my book.
         B♭
Turn the pages nice and slow.
      F
Look at pictures as you go.
    C   F
Take a look, take a look at my book.

Elizabeth McKinnon

Here Is a Box
Sung to: *Twinkle, Twinkle, Little Star*

C   F   C
Here is a box where something hides.
   (Make a fist with thumb inside.)
G₇   C   G₇   C
What do you think might be inside?
   (Cover fist with opposite hand.)
  C   F   C   G₇
A clown's inside. Should we open the top?
   (Lift hand and peek under it.)
C   F   C   G₇
Open it wide and out he will pop.
   (Remove hand and pop out thumb.)
C   F   C
Now let's close the lid up tight,
   (Make a fist with thumb inside.)
     G₇   C   G₇   C
And hold it shut with all our might.
   (Cover fist with opposite hand.)

Repeat, each time letting your children suggest a different word for *clown*.

Laura Egge
Lake Oswego, OR

20 Language Time

Wishing Song
Sung to: *Jimmy Crack Corn*

F   C₇
What does Jon wish that he could be?
   (Child responds.)

                                 F
He wishes that he could be a _____.
            B♭
That's what he wishes that he could be.
   C₇   F
And that is what he wishes.

Sing the song for each of your children.

Laura Egge
Lake Oswego, OR

Silly Rhymes
Sung to: *The Paw-Paw Patch*

 F
I saw a cat sitting on a hat.
  C₇
I saw a goat wearing a coat.
 F
I saw a whale swimming in a pail.
  C₇
Way down yonder
          F
In the paw-paw patch.

Continue with similar verses, letting your children help make up rhyming lines, such as *I saw a dog living with a hog* or *I saw a bear combing its hair.*

Laura Egge
Lake Oswego, OR

One Silly Boy
Sung to: *Three Blind Mice*

C   G₇   C   G₇   C
One silly boy, one silly boy.
        G₇   C   G₇   C
Always dressed wrong, never dressed right.
            G₇   C
He wore his shoes on his hands, you see.
           G₇   C
He wore his hat upon his knee.
            G₇   C
His shirt was where his pants should be.
    G₇   C
One silly boy.

Laura Egge
Lake Oswego, OR

Silly Song
Sung to: *Skip to My Lou*

F
What is that on your toe?
C₇
That's a hippo on my toe.
F
Do you want it on your toe?
  C₇   F
No, no, please get it off me!

F
What is that on your hand?
C₇
That's a butterfly on my hand.
F
Do you want it on your hand?
  C₇   F
Yes, yes, I like it on me!

Repeat, substituting the names of other body parts for *toe* and *hand* and letting your children suggest other words for *hippo* and *butterfly.*

Laura Egge
Lake Oswego, OR

M-u-s-i-c
Sung to: *Bingo*

       F   Bb   F
What makes us dance and clap and sing?
          C   F
Yes, music is its name-o.
    Bb   C   Bb   Bb
M-u-s-i-c, M-u-s-i-c, M-u-s-i-c.
        C   F
Yes, music is its name-o.

Diane Thom
Maple Valley, WA

Instrument Song
Sung to: *Mary Had a Little Lamb*

C
Triangles are playing,
G₇   C
Playing, playing.

Triangles are playing
G₇   C
In our little band.

Additional verses: Rhythm sticks are playing; Jingle bells are playing; Tambourines are playing; Little drums are playing; Shakers are playing.

Margery A. Kranyik
Hyde Park, MA

Our Marching Band
Sung to: *The Paw-Paw Patch*

F
One little, two little,

Three little instruments,
C₇
Four little, five little,

Six little instruments,
F
Seven little, eight little,

Nine little instruments
C₇
Playing loud and clear
      F
In our marching band.

Have your children play instruments on each number as you sing the song.

Margery A. Kranyik
Hyde Park, MA

When the Band Comes Marching By
Sung to: *When the Saints Go Marching In*

                 C
Oh, when the band comes marching by,
                                G₇
Oh, when the band comes marching by,
              C   F
We will play and sing and be happy
  C   G₇   C
When the band comes marching by.

Margery A. Kranyik
Hyde Park, MA

Instrument Sounds

Sung to: *The Mulberry Bush*

D
This is the sound the little drums make,
A₇
Little drums make, little drums make.
D
This is the sound the little drums make.
A₇   D
Listen to them now.
   (Beat drum three times.)

Continue with similar verses, substituting words, such as *shakers, little bells,* or *rhythm sticks,* for *little drums.*

Margery A. Kranyik
Hyde Park, MA

I Play My Horn

Sung to: *Up on the Housetop*

F
I play my horn with a toot-toot-toot.
B♭   F   C₇
Don't you think that it is cute?
F
I play my drum with a rum-pum-pum.
B♭   F   C   F
Don't you think it's a happy drum?
B♭   Aₘ   D₇
Toot-toot-toot, rum-pum-pum.
Gₘ   C₇   F
Toot-toot-toot, rum-pum-pum.
              B♭ F Bdim
All come along and join the fun,
F   Gₘ   C₇   F
While I play my horn and drum.

Margo S. Miller
Westerville, OH

The More We Play Together

Sung to: *Did You Ever See a Lassie?*

         F
The more we play together,
      C₇   F
Together, together,

The more we play together,
        C₇   F
The happier we sound.
     C₇   F
The drums and the shakers,
     C₇   F
The sticks and the bells.

The more we play together,
        C₇   F
The happier we sound.

Margery A. Kranyik
Hyde Park, MA

Cooking Song
Sung to: *The Paw-Paw Patch*

F
Beat the egg until it's smooth,
C₇
Beat the egg until it's smooth,
F
Beat the egg until it's smooth.
C₇
Cooking with my friends
F
At our school today.

Sing a verse for each step in the recipe you are preparing such as *Sift the flour and baking powder, Mix the butter with the sugar,* or *Spread the batter in the pan.*

Kristine Wagoner
Puyallup, WA

If You Want to Have a Snack
Sung to: *If You're Happy and You Know It*

    F   C
If you want to have a snack, wash your hands.
   (Pretend to wash hands.)
    C   F
If you want to have a snack, wash your hands.
   (Pretend to wash hands.)
    B♭
Use a little soap and water,
    F
It's not really such a bother.
    C   F
If you want to have a snack, wash your hands.
   (Pretend to wash hands.)

Phyllis Martinelli
Ooylestown, OH

Setting the Table
Sung to: *The Mulberry Bush*

D
This is the way we set the table,
A₇
Set the table, set the table.
D
This is the way we set the table
A₇   D
When it's time for a snack.

D
This is where we put the plates,
A₇
Put the plates, put the plates.
D
This is where we put the plates
A₇   D
When it's time for a snack.

Continue with similar verses, each time substituting a different word, such as *spoons* or *bowls,* for *plates.*

Elizabeth McKinnon

Time to Eat Our Snack

Sung to: *She'll Be Coming Round the Mountain*

     F
Oh, it's time to eat our snack now—

Yum, yum, yum!

Oh, it's time to eat our snack now—
C₇
Yum, yum, yum!
       F
Oh, we're having milk today,
   B♭
And we think that that's okay.
     F   C₇
Oh, it's time to eat our snack now—
F
Yum, yum, yum!

Substitute the name of a snack food you are serving for *milk*.

Laura Egge
Lake Oswego, OR

Eat Them Up

Sung to: *Frere Jacques*

C
Eat them up, eat them up,

Little Chad, little Chad.

Carrots and peas,

Very, very tasty!

Eat them up, eat them up.

Substitute the name of one of your children for *Chad* and the foods he or she is eating for *carrots and peas*.

Michelle Monoc
Kent, OH

I Like to Eat

Sung to: *Skip to My Lou*

F
I like to eat crackers and cheese.
C₇
I like to eat crackers and cheese.
F
I like to eat crackers and cheese.
C₇   F
Yum-yummy-yum-yum-yum!

Repeat, each time letting your children substitute names of different foods for *crackers and cheese*.

Barbara Backer
Charleston, SC

My Sipping Straw
Sung to: *The Muffin Man*

G
Watch me use my sipping straw,
  C   D₇
My sipping straw, my sipping straw.
G
Watch me use my sipping straw
  D₇   G
To sip and sip and sip.

 G
I use my straw to sip my juice,
C   D₇
Sip my juice, sip my juice.
G
I use my straw to sip my juice.
  D₇   G
I sip and sip and sip.

Repeat, substituting *milk* for *juice*.

Elizabeth McKinnon

Going on a Picnic
Sung to: *Did You Ever See a Lassie?*

            F
We are going on a picnic,
  C₇   F
A picnic, a picnic.

We are going on a picnic.
  C₇   F
Oh, what will you bring?
  C₇   F
Jill's bringing a sandwich.
  C₇   F
Abe's bringing some orange juice.

We are going on a picnic.
  C₇   F
Oh, what will you bring?

Substitute the names of your children and their chosen picnic foods for those in the song. Repeat until each child has been named.

Laura Egge
Lake Oswego, OR

Color Foods
Sung to: *Mary Had a Little Lamb*

C
I can eat a food that's red.
G₇   C
Good to eat, what a treat!

A food that's red is a strawberry.
G₇   C
Yum, yum, yum, yum, yum.

Sing the song for each of your children, letting the child choose the color and food he or she wants to sing about.

Barbara Backer
Charleston, SC

26 Snack Time

If You're Tired and You Know It
Sung to: *If You're Happy and You Know It*

       F   C
If you're tired and you know it, take a nap.
       C   F
If you're tired and you know it, take a nap.
       B♭
If you're tired and you know it,
            F
Then your eyes will surely show it.
       C   F
If you're tired and you know it, take a nap.

Stefanie Bair
Kent, OH

Close Your Eyes
Sung to: *Frere Jacques*

C
Kyle is sleepy, Kyle is sleepy.

Close your eyes, close your eyes.

It's time to go to sleep now.

Let's not hear a peep now.

Rest well, Kyle. Rest well, Kyle.

Sing the song for each of your children, substituting the child's name for *Kyle*.

Laura Egge
Lake Oswego, OR

A Sleepy Bear
Sung to: *Yankee Doodle*

  C   G₇
A sleepy bear crawls in its cave
    C   G₇
And sleeps all winter long.
    C   F
But Jane will take just a little nap,
   G₇   C
As soon as we finish this song.

Sing the song for each of your children, substituting the child's name for *Jane*.

Laura Egge
Lake Oswego, OR

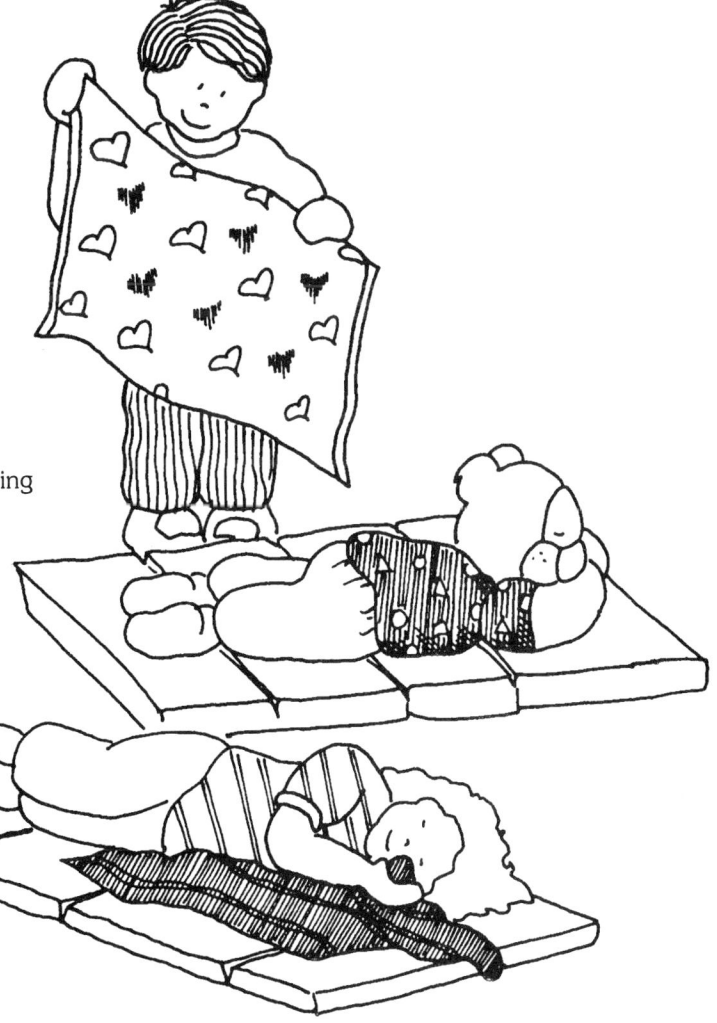

Ready for Bed
Sung to: *Twinkle, Twinkle, Little Star*

 C   F   C
Here is Teddy ready for bed.
G$_7$ C   G$_7$ C
Lay him down and rest his head.
C   F   C   G$_7$
Cover him up so he won't peep.
C   F   C   G$_7$
Watch him till he's fast asleep.
C   F   C
Here is Teddy ready for bed.
G$_7$ C   G$_7$ C
Lay him down and rest his head.

Give your children a teddy bear or a similar toy to "sing to sleep" at nap time.

Adapted Traditional

Hush, Little Dolly
Sung to: *Hush, Little Baby*

F   C$_7$
Hush, little dolly, don't you cry.
                  F
I'm going to sing you a lullaby.
            C$_7$
If you nap with me today,
                F
I'll wake you later so we can play.

Give each of your children a doll or a stuffed toy to sing to at nap time.

Laura Egge
Lake Oswego, OR

28 Nap Time

Monkey See and Do
Sung to: *Twinkle, Twinkle, Little Star*

C   F   C
Monkey see and monkey do.
G_7 C G_7 C
Monkey does the same as you.
C   F   C G_7
We are watching what you do.
C   F   C G_7
And we do the same thing, too.
C   F   C
Monkey see and monkey do.
G_7 C G_7 C
Monkey does the same as you.

Each time you sing the song, let one of your children make movements and have the others imitate him or her.

Laura Egge
Lake Oswego, OR

Everyone Hold Hands
Sung to: *The Farmer in the Dell*

D
Everyone hold hands.

Let go and turn around.

Shake your shoulders back and forth.
A_7 D
Then bend and touch the ground.

D
Reach up and touch the sky.

Stretch up so very high.

Touch your toes, then touch your nose.
A_7 D
Reach up and touch the sky.

Juanita Veeley
Louisville, KY

We Are Leaping
Sung to: *Frere Jacques*

C
We are leaping, we are leaping.

Leap, leap, leap. Leap, leap, leap.

Now let's all start twirling,

Now let's all start twirling.

Twirl, twirl, twirl. Twirl, twirl, twirl.

C
We are crawling, we are crawling.

Crawl, crawl, crawl. Crawl, crawl, crawl.

Now let's all start rolling,

Now let's all start rolling.

Roll, roll, roll. Roll, roll, roll.

Continue with similar verses, substituting other movements for those in the song.

Laura Egge
Lake Oswego, OR

Clap Your Hands

Sung to: *Row, Row, Row Your Boat*

C
Clap, clap, clap your hands
   (Clap and sing slowly.)

As slowly as can be.

Clap them, clap them,

Clap them, clap them.
G   C
Do it now with me.

C
Clap, clap, clap your hands
   (Clap and sing fast.)

As fast as fast can be.

Clap them, clap them,

Clap them, clap them.
G   C
Do it now with me.

Additional verses: Roll, roll, roll your hands; Wave, wave, wave your hands; Stomp, stomp, stomp your feet; Tap, tap, tap your toes.

Adapted Traditional

Stretch, Jump, and Bend

Sung to: *Twinkle, Twinkle, Little Star*

C   F   C
Stretching, stretching way up high,
   (Stretch.)
G₇   C   G₇   C
Stretching, stretching to the sky.
C   G₇   C   G₇
Stretching out and stretching in,
C   G₇   C   G₇
Stretching is how we begin.
C   F   C
Stretching, stretching way up high,
G₇   C   G₇   C
Stretching, stretching to the sky.

C   F   C
Jumping, jumping all around,
   (Jump.)
G₇   C   G₇   C
Jumping, jumping on the ground.
C   F   C   G₇
Jumping fast and jumping slow,
C   F   C   G₇
Jumping is the way to go.
C   F   C
Jumping, jumping all around,
G₇   C   G₇   C
Jumping, jumping on the ground.

C   F   C
Bending, bending, bend our knees,
   (Bend.)
G₇   C   G₇   C
Bending, bending—watch us, please.
C   F   C   G₇
Bending, bending way down low,
C   G₇   C   G₇
Bending's lots of fun, you know.
C   F   C
Bending, bending, bend our knees,
G₇   C   G₇   C
Bending, bending—watch us please.

Barbara B. Fleisher
Glen Oaks, NY

Here's a Game
Sung to: *Bingo*

F   B♭   F
Here's a game that's lots of fun,
          C   F
And this is how we play it.
      B♭
Hop, hop, hop, hop, hop.
    (Hop.)
C   F
Skip, skip, skip, skip, skip.
    (Skip.)
B♭
Turn, turn, turn, turn, turn.
    (Turn in a circle.)
      C   F
And that is how we play it.

Continue with similar verses, substituting other movements for those in the song.

*Laura Egge
Lake Oswego, OR*

Reach Up and Touch the Sky
Sung to: *If You're Happy and You Know It*

    F   C
Oh, I wish I could reach up and touch the sky.
    (Stretch arms high.)
   C   F
Oh, I wish I could reach up and touch the sky.
   B♭
Oh, if I could touch the sky,
   F
Then I'd get up there and fly.
    (Wave arms up and down.)
   C   F
Oh, I wish I could reach up and touch the sky.
    (Stretch arms high.)

*Laura Egge
Lake Oswego, OR*

Let's Pretend
Sung to: *Three Blind Mice*

C   G₇   C   G₇   C
Let's pretend, let's pretend.
C   G₇   C   G₇   C
What can I do, what can I do?
          G₇   C
I can crawl like a little crab,
    (Crawl around sideways.)
          G₇   C
I can crawl like a little crab,
          G₇   C
I can crawl like a little crab.
      G₇   C
Crawl, crawl, crawl.

C   G₇   C   G₇   C
Let's pretend, let's pretend.
        G₇   C   G₇   C
What can I do, what can I do?
         G₇   C
I can hop like a kangaroo,
    (Hop around.)
         G₇   C
I can hop like a kangaroo,
         G₇   C
I can hop like a kangaroo.
     G₇   C
Hop, hop, hop.

Continue with similar verses, such as *I can wiggle just like a worm* or *I can jump like a little frog.*

*Laura Egge
Lake Oswego, OR*

Movement Time

Time to Go Out and Play
Sung to: *The Bear Went Over the Mountain*

    D   G D
It's time to go out and play,
   A₇   D
It's time to go out and play,
                  G
It's time to go out and play
  A₇   D
With all our friends today.

Judy Hall
Wytheville, VA

It's Time to Go Outside
Sung to: *The Farmer in the Dell*

 D
It's time to go outside,

It's time to go outside.

Let's walk to the door.
  A₇   D
It's time to go outside.

Substitute a different action word, such as *skip*, *crawl*, or *tiptoe*, for *walk*.

Nadine Haskell
Kent, OH

I Love Sand
Sung to: *Three Blind Mice*

 C   G₇   C   G₇   C
Sand, sand, sand. Sand, sand, sand.
 G₇ C   G₇ C
I love sand, I love sand.
          G₇   C
It's fun to squish it between my toes,
         G₇   C
Or build a mountain as high as my nose,
        G₇   C
Or dig a tunnel that grows and grows,
      G₇   C
'Cause I love sand.

Susan Hodges

To the Playground Today
Sung to: *The Mulberry Bush*

     D
We're going to the playground today,
 A₇
Playground today, playground today.
     D
We're going to the playground today
  A₇   D
To play out in the sun.

D
Perhaps we'll play on the swings today,
A₇
Swings today, swings today.
D
Perhaps we'll play on the swings today.
  A₇   D
Let's go and have some fun.

Continue with similar verses, each time substituting the name of a different piece of playground equipment for *swings*.

Kathy McCullough
St. Charles, IL

32 Outdoor Time

The Swinging Song
Sung to: *Twinkle, Twinkle, Little Star*

C   F   C
Swing on your tummy, swing on your seat.
G_7 C G_7 C
Pump with your hands and knees and feet.
C   F   C G_7
Point your toes up in the air.
C   F   C G_7
Feel the wind blow through your hair.
C   F   C
When you're high up in a swing,
G_7 C G_7 C
You can do most anything!

Diane Thom
Maple Valley, WA

Riding on My Scooter
Sung to: *Little White Duck*

  F
I'm riding on my scooter,
       C
Watch me going past.

I'm riding on my scooter,
      F
Going very fast.
                  C
I like to ride around, you see.
                F
Riding's so much fun for me.

Oh, I'm riding on my scooter,
      C
Watch me going past.
 F
Going very fast!

Repeat, each time substituting the name of a different riding toy for *scooter*.

Gayle Bittinger

Sliding
Sung to: *Row, Row, Row Your Boat*

C
Climb, climb up the slide,
   (Sing slowly.)

Climb up to the top.

Sliding, sliding down the slide,
   (Sing fast.)
G   C
Slide until you stop.

Elizabeth McKinnon

Let's Clean Up
Sung to: *Frere Jacques*

C
Playtime's over, playtime's over.

Let's clean up, let's clean up.

Then we'll join the circle,

Then we'll join the circle

For more fun, for more fun.

Melissa Leonard
Minersville, PA

Oh Where, Oh Where Have My Helpers Gone?
Sung to: *Oh Where, Oh Where Has My Little Dog Gone?*

D   A₇
Oh where, oh where have my helpers gone?
                          D
I need some help right away.
              A₇
I don't want to do this job alone.
                                    D
Oh, helpers, please come my way!

Laura Egge
Lake Oswego, OR

This Is the Way
Sung to: *The Mulberry Bush*

D
This is the way we pick up toys,
A₇
Pick up toys, pick up toys.
D
This is the way we pick up toys.
       A₇   D
Our playtime now is over.

D
Rosie is picking up the blocks,
A₇
Up the blocks, up the blocks.
D
Rosie is picking up the blocks.
       A₇   D
Our playtime now is over.

D
Jason is putting the puzzles away,
A₇
Puzzles away, puzzles away.
D
Jason is putting the puzzles away.
       A₇   C
Our playtime now is over.

Sing a verse for each of your children, substituting the child's name and his or her cleanup activity for those in the song.

Laura Egge
Lake Oswego, OR

Pick Up Toys
Sung to: *Frere Jacques*

C
Girls and boys, girls and boys,

Pick up toys, pick up toys.

It's time to put the toys away.

Let's make it very clean today.

Thank you, all. Thank you, all.

Laura Egge
Lake Oswego, OR

Let's Put Our Toys Away
Sung to: *The Muffin Man*

G
Let's put all our toys away,
    C   D₇
Our toys away, our toys away.
G
Let's put all our toys away.
   D₇   G
Each in a special place!

Maria Courtright
Munroe Falls, OH

Playtime's Over
Sung to: *London Bridge*

C
Now it's time to pick up toys,
G₇   C
Pick up toys, pick up toys.

Now it's time to pick up toys.
G₇   C
Playtime's over.

C
Loni and Scott are cleaning up,
G₇   C
Cleaning up, cleaning up.

Loni and Scott are cleaning up.
G₇   C
Playtime's over.

Repeat, each time substituting the names of your children for those in the song.

Laura Egge
Lake Oswego, OR

We Are Cleaning
Sung to: *If You're Happy and You Know It*

       F   C
We are cleaning all the tables, watch us now.
       C   F
We are cleaning all the tables, we know how.
       B♭
We are scrubbing high and low.
       F
We are scrubbing fast and slow.
       C   F
We are cleaning all the tables, watch us now.

Repeat, each time substituting the name of the item your children are cleaning for *tables*.

Gayle Bittinger

Clean Up Earth
Sung to: *Frere Jacques*

C
Let's recycle, let's recycle.

Do it now, you know how.

Save your glass and pop cans,

Newspapers and pie pans.

Clean up earth, clean up earth.

Martha Thomas
Lake Clear, NY

Let's Recycle
Sung to: *London Bridge*

C
Separate the trash you have,
G₇   C
Trash you have, trash you have.

Separate the trash you have.
G₇   C
Let's recycle!

C
Plastic, paper, and glass jars,
G₇   C
And glass jars, and glass jars.

Plastic, paper, and glass jars.
G₇   C
Let's recycle!

C
Cans and boxes, newspapers,
G₇   C
Newspapers, newspapers.

Cans and boxes, newspapers.
G₇   C
Let's recycle!

Kim Chaney
Stillwater, OK

Our Friends
Sung to: *Mary Had a Little Lamb*

C
Taylor played on the slide today,
G₇   C
Slide today, slide today.

Taylor played on the slide today,
G₇   C
Taylor is our friend.

C
Gina was a helper today,
G₇   C
Helper today, helper today.

Gina was a helper today.
G₇   C
Gina is our friend.

C
Jamie played with Matt today,
G₇   C
Matt today, Matt today.

Jamie played with Matt today.
G₇   C
They are both our friends.

Sing similar verses for your children, substituting their names for those in the song.

*Laura Egge
Lake Oswego, OR*

Daddy Came to School
Sung to: *Yankee Doodle*

C   G₇
Daddy came to school today.
    C   G₇
He was my guest, you see.
    C   F
He found out what we do at school
         G₇   C
And had some fun with me.
    F
I showed him where I hang my coat
         C
And where we keep the toys.
F
Then I told him every name
            C   G₇   C
Of all the girls and boys!

Substitute an appropriate name, such as *Mommy* or *Grandma*, for *Daddy*.

*Deb Eschenbach
Fort Wayne, IN*

Our Day Is Done
Sung to: *The Farmer in the Dell*

D
Now our day is done.

We've all had lots of fun.

Tomorrow is another day,
               A₇   D
And we'll come back to play.

*Kerry L. Stanley
Centre Square, PA*

End of the Day

Time to Go Home Now

Sung to: *She'll Be Coming Round the Mountain*

     F
Oh, it's time to go on home now, so goodbye.

                                  C₇
Oh, it's time to go on home now, so goodbye.

    F
Well, it's been a lot of fun,

    B♭
But it's really time to run.

    F   C₇   F
Oh, it's time to go on home now, so goodbye.

Laura Egge
Lake Oswego, OR

Time to Say Goodbye

Sung to: *Skip to My Lou*

F
It's time to say goodbye.

C₇
It's time to say goodbye.

F
It's time to say goodbye.

   C₇   F
I'll see you all next time.

Laura Egge
Lake Oswego, OR

Wave Goodbye

Sung to: *Row, Row, Row Your Boat*

C
Wave, wave, wave your hands,

Wave them low and high.

Wave them, wave them, wave them, wave them
G   C
When you say goodbye.

Shana Sloan

38 End of the Day

Learning and Caring About Ourselves and Others

My Phone Number
Sung to: *The Muffin Man*

   G
Oh, do you know your phone number,
  (Adult sings.)

  C   D₇
Your phone number, your phone number?
  G
Oh, do you know your phone number?
 D₇   G
5-5-5–1-2-3-4.

   G
Oh, yes, I know my phone number,
  (Child responds.)

  C   D₇
My phone number, my phone number.
  G
Oh, yes, I know my phone number.
 D₇   G
5-5-5–1-2-3-4.

Sing the song for each of your children, substituting the child's phone number for the one in the song.

Laura Egge
Lake Oswego, OR

Who Are You?
Sung to: *Frere Jacques*

C
What's your name, what's your name?
  (Adult sings.)

Adam Smith, Adam Smith.
  (Child responds.)

What is your street?
  (Adult sings.)

What is your street?

Summit Drive, Summit Drive.
  (Child responds.)

Sing the song for each of your children.

Laura Egge
Lake Oswego, OR

Dial 9–1–1
Sung to: *London Bridge*

C
Dial 9–1–1 when you need help,
G₇   C
You need help, you need help.

Dial 9–1–1 when you need help.
G₇   C
They will help you.

If appropriate, substitute your community's emergency phone number for *9–1–1*.

Laura Egge
Lake Oswego, OR

Stop, Drop, and Roll
Sung to: *Skip to My Lou*

F
Stop, stop. Stop, drop, and roll,
C₇
Stop, stop. Stop, drop, and roll,
F
Stop, stop. Stop, drop, and roll
C₇   F
If your clothes catch on fire.

F
Don't run, whatever you do,
C₇
Don't run, whatever you do,
F
Don't run, whatever you do.
C₇   F
Just roll to put out the fire.

Let your children practice rolling on the floor as you sing the song.

Laura Egge
Lake Oswego, OR

Yucky, Blucky Mr. Yuk
Sung to: *Frere Jacques*

C
Mr. Yuk, Mr. Yuk,

You taste yucky, you taste blucky.

You are telling us to

Stay away from you!

Mr. Yuk, Mr. Yuk.

Lynn Cummisford
Waukesha, WI

We Stop, Look, and Listen
Sung to: *Row, Row, Row Your Boat*

C
We stop, look, and listen

Before we cross the street.

First we use our eyes and ears.
G   C
Then we use our feet.

Adapted Traditional

We Buckle Up

Sung to: *When Johnny Comes Marching Home*

Em
We like to travel in our car.
G
Hurrah, hurrah!
Em
Our car can take us near or far.
B
Hurrah, hurrah!
G   D
We buckle up before we go,
Em   B
Whether we're going fast or slow,
      Em Am Em B Em
So we'll all be safer riding in our car.

Vicki Shannon
Napton, MO

Carpentry Safety Song

Sung to: *The Mulberry Bush*

D
This is the way we use a saw,
   (Pretend to use a saw.)

A₇
Use a saw, use a saw.
D
This is the way we use a saw
A₇   D
When we use it safely.

Repeat, each time substituting the name of a different carpentry tool for *saw* and making appropriate movements.

Janice Bodenstedt
Jackson, MI

What Would You Do?

Sung to: *London Bridge*

C
What would you do if your house caught fire,
G₇   C
House caught fire, house caught fire?

What would you do if your house caught fire?
G₇   C
What would you do?
   (Encourage children to respond.)

Substitute similar phrases about other safety-related situations, such as *if your mom fell down* or *if a stranger offered a ride,* for *if your house caught fire.*

Laura Egge
Lake Oswego, OR

I'm a Healthy Person

Sung to: *I'm a Little Teapot*

C
I'm a healthy person
F   C
Walking down the street,
  (Walk around room.)
G₇   C
Swinging my arms
    G₇   C
And stretching my feet.
  (Swing arms and take big steps.)

I feel so good.
    F   C
My heart does, too.
  (Point to heart.)
F
Walk with me—
     G₇   C
It's good for you!

Jean Warren

Choose Foods That Are Good for You

Sung to: *The Battle Hymn of the Republic*

G
Choose foods that are good for you

At every meal you eat.
C
Choose foods that are good for you
    G
At every meal you eat.
G
Choose foods that are good for you

At every meal you eat,
    C   D₇   G
And you'll grow up big and strong.

G
Breads and grains and fruits and veggies,
C   G
Meats and beans are good choices.
G
Milk and cheese and yogurt, also,
C   D₇   G
Help you grow big and strong.

Priscilla M. Starrett
Warren, PA

Brushing Our Teeth

Sung to: *The Farmer in the Dell*

   D
We brush 'em in the morning,
  (Pretend to brush teeth.)

We brush 'em in the night.

Heigh-ho the derry-oh.
    A₇   D
We brush 'em till they're bright!

Sandy Coburn
Atwater, OH

Good Health Song
Sung to: *Row, Row, Row Your Boat*

C
Wash, wash, wash your body.
   (Pretend to wash body.)

Scrub and scrub and scrub.

Get yourself all sparkling clean,
G   C
When you're in the tub.

C
Brush, brush, brush your teeth.
   (Pretend to brush teeth.)

Make them shiny bright.

Do it every morning,
   G   C
And do it every night.

Laura Egge
Lake Oswego, OR

Let's Wash It and Kiss It
Sung to: *Oh Dear, What Can the Matter Be?*

C
Oh dear, what can the matter be?
G
Dear, dear, what can the matter be?
C
Oh dear, what can the matter be?
G   C
Molly fell down and got hurt.

C
Oh dear, let's wash it and kiss it.
G
Dear, dear, let's wash it and kiss it.
C
Oh dear, let's wash it and kiss it,
G   C
So Molly can go back and play.

Substitute the name of one of your children for *Molly*.

Laura Egge
Lake Oswego, OR

44 Health

Keep the Germs Away

Sung to: *The Mulberry Bush*

D
This is the way we wash our hands,
   (Pretend to wash hands.)

A₇
Wash our hands, wash our hands.

D
This is the way we wash our hands
   A₇   D
To keep the germs away.

D
This is the way we cover our sneezes,
   (Place hand over mouth.)

A₇
Cover our sneezes, cover our sneezes.

D
This is the way we cover our sneezes
   A₇   D
To keep the germs away.

D
This is the way we eat good foods,
   (Pretend to eat.)

A₇
Eat good foods, eat good foods.

D
This is the way we eat good foods
   A₇   D
To keep the germs away.

D
This is the way we get our rest,
   (Lay cheek on folded hands.)

A₇
Get our rest, get our rest.

D
This is the way we get our rest
   A₇   D
To keep the germs away.

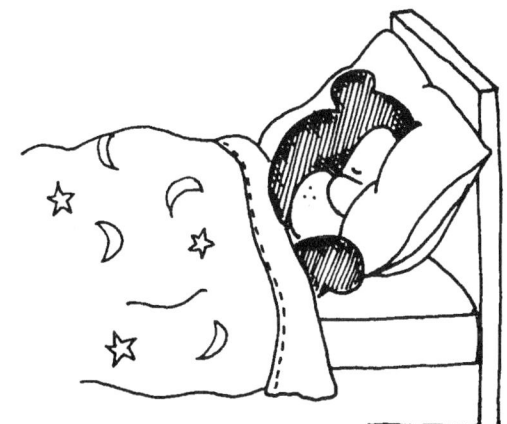

Susan M. Paprocki
Northbrook, IL

So Many Parts of Me
Sung to: *Twinkle, Twinkle, Little Star*

C　　　　　F　　C
On my face I have a nose.
G₇　　　　C　G₇　　C
On my feet I have ten toes.
C　　　F　　　C　　G₇
I've five fingers on each hand.
C　　F　　　C　　　　G₇
I've two legs that help me stand.
C　　　　　F　　　C
I have two eyes so I can see.
G₇　　　　C　G₇　　C
There are so many parts of me!

Diane Thom
Maple Valley, WA

My Eyes Can See
Sung to: *Twinkle, Twinkle, Little Star*

C　　　　　F　　　C
My eyes can see, my mouth can talk.
G₇　　　　C　G₇　　C
My ears can hear, my feet can walk.
C　　　F　　　C　　G₇
My nose can smell, my teeth can bite.
C　　G₇　　　C　　　G₇
My lids can blink, my hands can write.
C　　　　　F　　　C
These are some of the parts of me.
G₇　　　　C　G₇　　C
I know them well, as you can see.

Point to each body part mentioned as you sing the song.

Adapted Traditional

Eyes and Ears
Sung to: *Frere Jacques*

C
Eyes and ears, eyes and ears.

Mouth and nose, mouth and nose.

Can you see my eyes?

Can you see my ears?

And my mouth, and my nose?

Point to each body part mentioned as you sing the song.

Adapted Traditional

46 Body Parts

Body Joints Song

Sung to: *Frere Jacques*

C
Find your elbows, find your elbows.

Bend them now, this is how.
 (Bend elbows.)

Elbows bend your arm bones,

Elbows bend your arm bones.

Bend them now, bend them now.

C
Find your wrists, find your wrists.

Bend them now, this is how.
 (Bend wrists.)

Wrists bend your hand bones,

Wrists bend your hand bones.

Bend them now, bend them now.

C
Find your knees, find your knees.

Bend them now, this is how.
 (Bend knees.)

Knees bend your leg bones,

Knees bend your leg bones.

Bend them now, bend them now.

C
Find your ankles, find your ankles.

Bend them now, this is how.
 (Bend ankles.)

Ankles bend your foot bones,

Ankles bend your foot bones.

Bend them now, bend them now.

Betty Silkunas
Lansdale, PA

Mirror, Mirror
Sung to: *Twinkle, Twinkle, Little Star*

    C   F   C
I look in the mirror and who do I see?
(Pretend to look in a mirror.)

    G₇   C   G₇   C
A very wonderful, special me!
(Point to self.)

     C   F   C   G₇
With sparkling eyes all shiny and bright,
(Point to eyes.)

    C   F   C   G₇
My smile shows my teeth so pearly white.
(Show teeth in a smile.)

    C   F   C
It certainly is great to be
(Nod head.)

    G₇   C   G₇   C
This very wonderful, special me!
(Hug self.)

Ann M. O'Connell
Coaldale, PA

Special Me
Sung to: *Twinkle, Twinkle, Little Star*

    C   F   C
Special, special, special me.
(Point to self.)

    G₇   C   G₇   C
How I wonder what I'll be.
(Rest chin on folded hands.)

    C F   C   G₇
In the big world I can be
(Make circle with arms.)

    C   F   C   G₇
Anything I want to be.
(Nod head.)

    C   F   C
Special, special, special me.
(Point to self.)

    G₇   C   G₇   C
How I wonder what I'll be.
(Rest chin on folded hands.)

Kristine Wagoner
Puyallup, WA

You Are Special
Sung to: *Frere Jacques*

C
You are special, you are special.

That's for sure, that's for sure.

No one else is like you.

No one else is like you.

You're our friend, you're our friend.

Sing the song for each of your children.

Laura Egge
Lake Oswego, OR

A Special Person

Sung to: *Jimmy Crack Corn*

F   C₇
Alan is a special person,
        F
Alan is a special person,
       Bb
Alan is a special person.
  C₇   F
And that's why we like him.

Sing the song for each of your children, substituting the child's name for *Alan*.

Laura Egge
Lake Oswego, OR

All About Me

Sung to: *Twinkle, Twinkle, Little Star*

C   F   C
Let me tell you all about me.
G₇   C   G₇   C
I am special, you will see.
C   G₇   C   G₇
I can count and run and sing.
C   G₇   C   G₇
I can do most anything.
C   F   C
Let me tell you all about me.
G₇   C   G₇   C
I am special, you will see.

Repeat, encouraging your children to substitute their special talents for *count, run,* and *sing*.

Betty Silkunas
Lansdale, PA

I Like It

Sung to: *A-Tisket, A-Tasket*

C
I like it, I like it.

I like the way you did that.
  G₇
You put the toys back in the box.
        C
I like the way you did it.

Substitute an appropriate phrase, such as *you zipped your coat up by yourself* or *you painted with the purple paint,* for *you put the toys back in the box*.

Laura Egge
Lake Oswego, OR

Self-Esteem 49

So Many People Love You
Sung to: *Did You Ever See a Lassie?*

   F
So many people love you,
   C₇   F
They love you, they love you.

So many people love you,
   C₇   F
They love you so much.
   C₇   F
Like Mommy and Daddy
   C₇   F
And Grandma and Grandpa.
   F
So many people love you,
   C₇   F
They love you so much.

Repeat, substituting names your children suggest for *Mommy, Daddy, Grandma,* and *Grandpa.*

Laura Egge
Lake Oswego, OR

You Can, Too
Sung to: *Frere Jacques*

C
Laura is painting, Laura is painting.

You can, too, you can, too.

She's painting red and yellow,

She's painting red and yellow.

You can, too, you can, too.

C
Jacob is building, Jacob is building.

You can, too, you can, too.

He's building with the blocks,

He's building with the blocks.

You can, too, you can, too.

Substitute the names of your children and the things that they are doing for those in the song.

Gayle Bittinger

I Know How

Sung to: *If You're Happy and You Know It*

    F   C
Oh, I know how to put on my own shoes.
    (Pretend to put on shoes.)
    C   F
I can put on my own shirt, yes, it's true.
    (Pretend to put on shirt.)
    Bb
I know how to wash my face
    (Pretend to wash face.)
    F
And comb my hair back into place.
    (Pretend to comb hair.)
    C   F
Oh, look at all the things that I can do!

Becky Valenick
Rockford, IL

You Can Do It

Sung to: *London Bridge*

C
If you want to learn something new,
            G$_7$ C
Learn something new, learn something new,

If you want to learn something new,
G$_7$ C
Keep on trying!

C
If you practice, you will see,
G$_7$ C
You will see, you will see,

If you practice, you will see
G$_7$ C
You can do it!

Janice Bodenstedt
Jackson, MI

How I Feel

Sung to: *Twinkle, Twinkle, Little Star*

  C   F   C
Sometimes on my face you'll see
 G₇   C   G₇   C
How I feel inside of me.
   C   G₇   C   G₇
A smile means happy, a frown means sad.
   C   G₇   C   G₇
And when I grit my teeth I'm mad.
C   F   C
When I'm proud, I beam and glow,
  G₇   C   G₇   C
But when I'm shy, my head hangs low.

Karen Folk
Franklin, MA

Tell Me How You Feel

Sung to: *Skip to My Lou*

F
Show me how you look when you're mad.
C₇
Show me how you look when you're sad.
F
Show me how you look when you're glad.
     C₇   F
Then tell me how you feel now.

Sing the song for each of your children.

Laura Egge
Lake Oswego, OR

I'll Hug You

Sung to: *The Farmer in the Dell*

   D
I'll hug you when you're sad.

I'll hug you when you're glad.

I'll hug you when you're feeling scared.
  A₇   D
I'll hug you when you're mad.

Betty Silkunas
Lansdale, PA

We Know How to Get Along
Sung to: *Mary Had a Little Lamb*

C
We know how to get along,
G₇   C
Get along, get along.

We know how to get along
G₇   C
Every single day.

C
We take turns and share a lot,
G₇   C
Share a lot, share a lot.

We take turns and share a lot
G₇   C
While we work and play.

Kathy McCullough
St. Charles, IL

Sharing
Sung to: *Row, Row, Row Your Boat*

C
Share, share, share the toys.

It's so much fun to share.

I share with you, you share with me.
      G   C
We share because we care.

Elizabeth McKinnon

We Are Helpers
Sung to: *This Old Man*

C
We are pals as we play,
F   G₇
Helpers sharing every day.
                 C
With a "May I help?" and a "Thank you," too.
G₇   C   G₇   C
We are helpers through and through.

Margery A. Kranyik
Hyde Park, MA

Share Our Toys
Sung to: *Row, Row, Row Your Boat*

C
Let's all share our toys.

Let's share them with our friends.

It's so much fun to share our toys.
   G   C
Sharing has no end.

Rosemary Giordano
Philadelphia, PA

Sharing and Caring

Cooperation

Sung to: *Yankee Doodle*

C   G₇
Cooperation is the thing
C   G₇
We all must learn to do.
C   F
It makes life so very nice
G₇   C
And gets the work done, too.
F
Let's cooperate today
C
In our work and play.
        F
Who knows what we can get done
C   G₇   C
If we all work this way!

Jean Warren

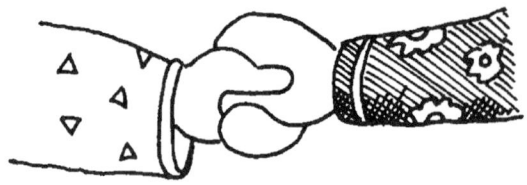

Kind Words

Sung to: *Skip to My Lou*

      F
It's nice to say, "Thank you."
      C₇
It's nice to say, "Thank you."
      F
It's nice to say, "Thank you,"
      C₇   F
When someone's kind to you.

      F
It's nice to say, "Excuse me."
      C₇
It's nice to say, "Excuse me."
      F
It's nice to say, "Excuse me,"
C₇   F
When you cough or sneeze.

      F
It's nice to say, "Please."
      C₇
It's nice to say, "Please."
      F
It's nice to say, "Please,"
C₇   F
When you ask for help.

Judith Taylor Burtchet
El Dorado, KS

These Little Words

Sung to: *London Bridge*

    C
These little words can make you smile,
G₇   C
Make you smile, make you smile.

These little words can make you smile—
G₇   C
Please and *thank you.*

Betty Silkunas
Lansdale, PA

Talking to People

Sung to: *Did You Ever See a Lassie?*

         F
When you talk to people,
     C₇   F
You should use good manners.

When you talk to people,
     C₇   F
You should be polite.
    C₇   F
When they say, "Thank you,"
    C₇   F
Then you say, "You're welcome."

When you talk to people,
    C₇   F
You should be polite.

         F
When you talk to people,
    C₇   F
You should use good manners.

When you talk to people,
    C₇   F
You should be polite.
    C₇   F
When they say, "How are you?"
    C₇   F
Then you say, "Fine, thank you."

When you talk to people,
    C₇   F
You should be polite.

Jean D. Smith
Huron, OH

Counting Friends
Sung to: *London Bridge*

C
How many friends are here today,
G₇   C
Here to work, here to play?

How many friends are here today?
G₇   C
Let's all count them.
   (Count.)

Betty Silkunas
Lansdale, PA

All Our Friends
Sung to: *Camptown Races*

C
All our friends are here today.
G₇
Hurray, hurray!
C
All our friends are here today,
G₇   C
Here to work and play.

Friends can help us smile
F   C
All along the way.

I'll be your friend and you'll be mine.
G₇   C
Happy, happy day!

Margery A. Kranyik
Hyde Park, MA

Friends
Sung to: *ABC Song*

C   F   C
Friends are big, friends are small.
G₇   C   G₇   C
Friends will help you if you fall.
C   F   C   G₇
Friends are happy, friends are sad.
C   F   C   G₇
Friends can make each other glad.

C   F   C
Friends are short, friends are tall.
G₇   C   G₇   C
Friends are happy when you call.
C   F   C
Friends are young, friends are old.
G₇   C   G₇   C
Friends are worth much more than gold.

C   G₇   C   G₇
Friends are near, friends are far.
C   G₇   C   G₇
Friends will like you as you are.
C   F   C
Friends are dark, friends are light.
G₇   C   G₇   C
Friends will bring you much delight!

Jean Warren

I Have a Friend
Sung to: *The Mulberry Bush*

D
I have a friend who plays with me,
A₇
Plays with me, plays with me.
D
I have a friend who plays with me.
A₇   D
Here's what we like to do.

D
We like to stack the blocks up high,
A₇
Blocks up high, blocks up high.
D
We like to stack the blocks up high.
A₇   D
That's what we like to do.

D
We like to play with the big dump truck,
A₇
Big dump truck, big dump truck.
D
We like to play with the big dump truck.
A₇   D
That's what we like to do.

Continue with similar verses about things your children like to do with their friends.

Elizabeth McKinnon

A Friend of Mine
Sung to: *Mary Had a Little Lamb*

C
Hannah is a friend of mine,
G₇   C
Friend of mine, friend of mine.

Yes, indeed, I like her fine!
G₇   C
She is a friend of mine.

Sing the song for each of your children, substituting the child's name for *Hannah*.

Louanne Hutcheson
Carrollton, GA

With All My Friends
Sung to: *She'll Be Coming Round the Mountain*

F
Oh, I like to go to school with all my friends.
                                        C₇
Oh, I like to go to school with all my friends.
F
There is Tonya, Luis, Eric,
        B♭
And there's Keisha, Garth, and Emily.
F   C₇   F
Oh, I like to go to school with all my friends.

Substitute the names of your children for those in the song and repeat until each child has been mentioned.

Barbara Backer
Charleston, SC

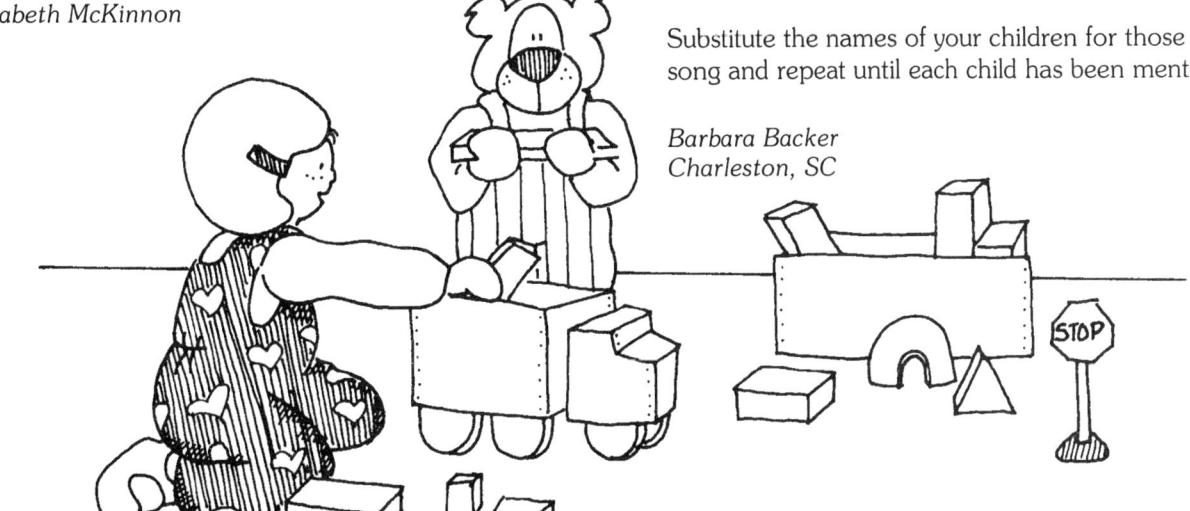

Friends 57

Together

Sung to: *Did You Ever See a Lassie?*

    F   C₇   F
The more we learn together, together, together,
                     C₇   F
The more we learn together, the happier we'll be.
    C₇   F
For my school is your school,
        C₇   F
And your school is my school.
                     C₇   F
The more we learn together, the happier we'll be.

    F   C₇   F
The more we share together, together, together,
                    C₇   F
The more we share together, the happier we'll be.
    C₇   F
For my toys are your toys,
        C₇   F
And your toys are my toys.
                   C₇   F
The more we share together, the happier we'll be.

    F   C₇   F
The more we play together, together, together,
                  C₇   F
The more we play together, the happier we'll be.
    C₇   F
For my friends are your friends,
        C₇   F
And your friends are my friends.
                 C₇   F
The more we play together, the happier we'll be.

    F   C₇   F
The more we smile together, together, together,
                  C₇   F
The more we smile together, the happier we'll be.
    C₇   F
For my smile's a big smile,
        C₇   F
And your smile's a big smile.
                 C₇   F
The more we smile together, the happier we'll be.

Margery A. Kranyik
Hyde Park, MA

Concepts

Five Colors Song
Sung to: *Three Blind Mice*

C   G₇ C   G₇   C
Red, red, red. Red, red, red.
      G₇ C   G₇ C
What is red, what is red?
             G₇   C
An apple, a rose, and a strawberry,
       G₇   C
Cherries growing on a tree,
           G₇   C
My nose on a day cold and frosty—
   G₇   C
They all are red.

C   G₇   C   G₇   C
Yellow, yellow, yellow. Yellow, yellow, yellow.
      G₇ C   G₇ C
What is yellow, what is yellow?
        G₇   C
A school bus parked at a school bus stop,
       G₇   C
Bananas grown in a land that's hot,
      G₇   C
Daffodils bright in a garden spot—
   G₇   C
They all are yellow.

C   G₇ C   G₇ C
Blue, blue, blue. Blue, blue, blue.
     G₇ C   G₇ C
What is blue, what is blue?
       G₇   C
The sea, the sky, and some people's eyes,
        G₇   C
Blueberries picked for a scrumptious pie,
      G₇   C
A bluebird flying away up high—
   G₇ C
They all are blue.

C   G₇   C   G₇   C
Green, green, green. Green, green, green.
     G₇ C   G₇ C
What is green, what is green?
        G₇   C
Grass and plants and trees and leaves,
       G₇   C
Lettuce we put in the salad we eat,
         G₇   C
Grasshoppers hopping around our feet—
   G₇ C
They all are green.

C   G₇   C   G₇   C
Orange, orange, orange. Orange, orange, orange.
     G₇ C   G₇ C
What is orange, what is orange?
       G₇   C
An orange, a cantaloupe, and a peach,
       G₇   C
A pumpkin, a goldfish, and Cheddar cheese,
      G₇   C
The carrot that my little rabbit eats—
   G₇ C
They all are orange.

Diane Thom
Maple Valley, WA

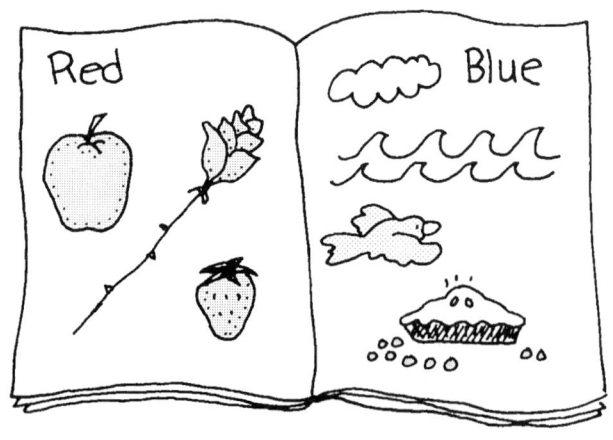

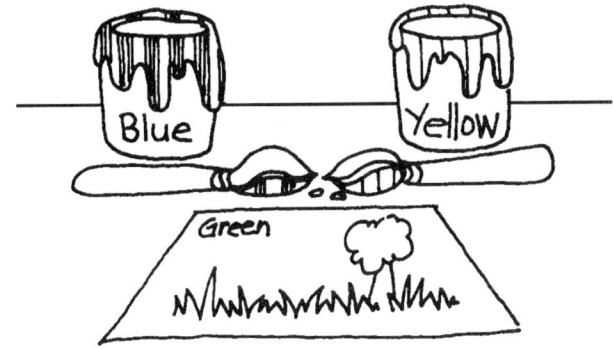

Blue and Yellow

Sung to: *If You're Happy and You Know It*

      F   C
Blue and yellow mixed together will make green,
     C   F
Like the grass or a skinny, long string bean,
      Bb
Like a pickle or a lime.
    F
Yes, I promise every time,
     C   F
If you mix blue and yellow, you'll make green.

Diane Thom
Maple Valley, WA

Yellow and Red

Sung to: *Twinkle, Twinkle, Little Star*

C   F   C
Yellow and red, yellow and red.
G₇   C   G₇   C
Mix them—orange is what you'll get.
C   F   C   G₇
Orange is the color of a fruit you eat
C   F   C   G₇
Or a construction cone in the street.
C   F   C
Yellow and red, yellow and red.
G₇   C   G₇   C
Mix them—orange is what you'll get.

Diane Thom
Maple Valley, WA

Red and Blue

Sung to: *Twinkle, Twinkle, Little Star*

C   F   C
Red and blue, red and blue.
G₇   C   G₇   C
Mix them up, there's purple for you.
C   F   C   G₇
Purple like cabbage we sometimes eat.
C   F   C   G₇
Purple like plums that taste so sweet.
C   F   C
Red and blue, red and blue.
G₇   C   G₇   C
Mix them up, there's purple for you.

Diane Thom
Maple Valley, WA

Black and White

Sung to: *Twinkle, Twinkle, Little Star*

C   F   C
Mixing black and white today,
G₇   C   G₇   C
We will make the color gray.
C   F   C   G₇
Gray like concrete for the street.
C   F   C   G₇
Gray like clay or elephant feet.
C   F   C
Mixing black and white today,
G₇   C   G₇   C
We will make the color gray.

Diane Thom
Maple Valley, WA

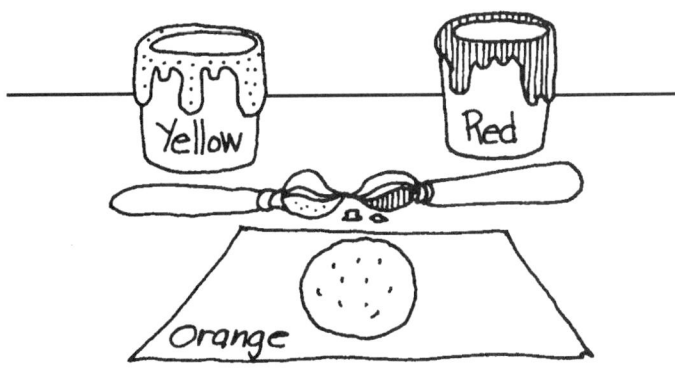

Colors That We Know
Sung to: *Twinkle, Twinkle, Little Star*

C   F   C
Yellow sunshine, soft green grass,
G₇   C   G₇   C
Orange goldfish, small black bats.
C   G₇   C   G₇
Blue cold water, purple plums,
C   G₇   C   G₇
Red strawberries—yum, yum, yum!
C   F   C
Big brown tree trunks, bright white snow.
G₇   C   G₇   C
These are colors that we know.

Diane Thom
Maple Valley, WA

Where Are the Colors?
Sung to: *The Paw-Paw Patch*

F
Where, oh, where are the kids with blue on?
C₇
Where, oh, where are the kids with blue on?
F
Where, oh, where are the kids with blue on?
C₇   F
Stand up tall so we can see you now.

Repeat, each time substituting a different color for *blue* and a different action for *stand up tall.*

Ann-Marie Donovan
Framingham, MA

If You're Wearing Red Today
Sung to: *If You're Happy and You Know It*

            F   C
If you're wearing red today, nod your head.
            C   F
If you're wearing red today, nod your head.
           Bb
If you're wearing red today,
         F
Nod your head and shout hurray.
            C   F
If you're wearing red today, nod your head.

Additional verses: If you're wearing blue today, tap your toe; If you're wearing yellow today, raise your hand; If you're wearing orange today, clap your hands; If you're wearing green today, stand up tall.

June Meckel
Andover, MA

 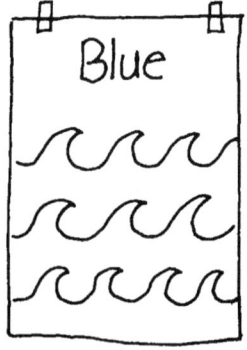

A Circle

Sung to: *Did You Ever See a Lassie?*

       F
Did you ever see a circle,
 C₇   F
A circle, a circle?

Did you ever see a circle?
 C₇   F
It looks like a ball.
 C₇   F
It looks like a ball,
 C₇   F
It looks like a ball.

Did you ever see a circle?
 C₇   F
It looks like a ball.

Substitute a different word, such as *plate*, for *ball*.

Priscilla M. Starrett
Warren, PA

A Square

Sung to: *Did You Ever See a Lassie?*

       F
Did you ever see a square,
 C₇   F
A square, a square?

Did you ever see a square?
 C₇   F
It looks like a box.
 C₇   F
It looks like a box,
 C₇   F
It looks like a box.

Did you ever see a square?
 C₇   F
It looks like a box.

Substitute a different word, such as *cube*, for *box*.

Priscilla M. Starrett
Warren, PA

I Can Make a Shape

Sung to: *Skip to My Lou*

F
I can make a square, how about you?
C₇
I can make a square, how about you?
F
I can make a square, how about you?
C₇   F
Make a little square just like I do.
   (Form square with fingers.)

Additional verses: I can make a circle; a triangle; a rectangle.

Jean Warren

Shapes

A Rectangle
Sung to: *Did You Ever See a Lassie?*

    F
Did you ever see a rectangle,
  C₇   F
A rectangle, a rectangle?

Did you ever see a rectangle?
  C₇   F
It looks like a book.
  C₇   F
It looks like a book,
  C₇   F
It looks like a book.

Did you ever see a rectangle?
  C₇   F
It looks like a book.

Substitute a different word, such as *door,* for *book.*

Priscilla M. Starrett
Warren, PA

A Triangle
Sung to: *Did You Ever See a Lassie?*

    F
Did you ever see a triangle,
  C₇   F
A triangle, a triangle?

Did you ever see a triangle?
  C₇   F
It looks like a sail.
  C₇   F
It looks like a sail,
  C₇   F
It looks like a sail.

Did you ever see a triangle?
  C₇   F
It looks like a sail.

Substitute a different word, such as *tent,* for *sail.*

Priscilla M. Starrett
Warren, PA

Sing a Song of Shapes
Sung to: *Sing a Song of Sixpence*

G
Sing a song of shapes.
D
Find them everywhere.

Sing a song of shapes.
G
Draw them in the air.

When you look for shapes
C
Hiding all around,
D
You will see a lot of shapes
            G
Are waiting to be found!

Gayle Bittinger

Draw a Circle
Sung to: *Frere Jacques*

C
Draw a circle, draw a circle

Round as can be, round as can be.

Draw a circle,

Draw a circle

Just for me, just for me.
   (Draw circle in air with finger.)

C
Draw a rectangle, draw a rectangle

Shaped like a door, shaped like a door.

Draw a retangle,

Draw a retangle

With corners four, with corners four.
   (Draw rectangle in air with finger.)

C
Draw a triangle, draw a triangle

With corners three, with corners three.

Draw a triangle,

Draw a triangle

Just for me, just for me.
   (Draw triangle in air with finger.)

Adapted Traditional

Shapes Movement Song
Sung to: *Skip to My Lou*

F
Jump, jump, jump to the circle.

C₇
Jump, jump, jump to the circle.

F
Jump, jump, jump to the circle.

C₇   F
Jump to the circle right now.
   (Clap.)

F
Run, run, run to the square.

C₇
Run, run, run to the square.

F
Run, run, run to the square.

C₇   F
Run to the square right now.
   (Clap.)

F
Roll, roll, roll to the triangle.

C₇
Roll, roll, roll to the triangle.

F
Roll, roll, roll to the triangle.

C₇   F
Roll to the triangle right now.
   (Clap.)

Before singing the song, tape a large paper circle, square, and triangle to the floor.

Sue Yanchar
Kent, OH

Shapes **65**

One, Two, Three
Sung to: *This Old Man*

C
One, two, three, count with me.
F   G₇
It's as easy as can be—

Four, five, six, seven, eight, nine, ten.
G₇   C   G₇   C
Now let's sing it once again.

Judy Hall
Wytheville, VA

Clap One, Two, Three
Sung to: *Row, Row, Row Your Boat*

C
Clap, clap, clap your hands,

Clap them one, two, three.

The more you clap, the more we count.
G   C
So what will your count be?

C
One, two, three, four,

Five, six, seven.

The more you clap, the more we count.
G   C
Eight, nine, ten, eleven.

Adapted Traditional

I Can Count
Sung to: *Frere Jacques*

C
I can count, I can count.

One, two, three, one, two, three.

I can count higher,

I can count higher.

Four, five, six, four, five, six.

C
I can count, I can count.

One, two, three, four, five, six.

I can count higher,

I can count higher.

Seven, eight, nine, seven, eight, nine.

C
I can count, I can count.

One, two, three, four, five, six.

I can count higher,

I can count higher.

Seven, eight, nine, ten, eleven, twelve.

Saundra Winnett
Lewisville, TX

Ten Little Toes
Sung to: *This Old Man*

C
I've got toes

On my feet.
F
Ten little toes,
   G₇
Now, aren't they sweet?
  C
Let's count them now,

All the way to ten.
G₇
Then we'll count
  C G₇   C
All over again.

Margo S. Miller
Westerville, OH

Four Number Birds
Sung to: *Twinkle, Twinkle, Little Star*

C   F   C
One little bird flying in the blue.
   (Hold up one finger.)
    G₇   C   G₇   C
Along comes another, now there are two.
   (Hold up two fingers.)
C   G₇   C   G₇
Two little birds perched high in a tree.
C   G₇   C   G₇
Along comes another, now there are three.
   (Hold up three fingers.)
C   F   C
Three little birds, see them swoop and soar.
  G₇   C   G₇   C
Along comes another, and that makes four.
   (Hold up four fingers.)

Diane Thom
Maple Valley, WA

One Rap, Two Rap
Sung to: *Skip to My Lou*

F
One rap, two rap, three rap, four.
   (Rap fist.)
C₇
Who's that rapping at my door?
F
Five rap, six rap, seven rap, eight.
   (Rap fist.)
C₇   F
Don't you think it's kind of late?

Jean Warren

Numbers **67**

ABC Song

Sung to: *Twinkle, Twinkle, Little Star*

 C   F   C
A is for alligator, airplane, and ants.
G₇   C   G₇   C
A is for astronaut doing a dance.
 C   G₇   C   G₇
B is for ball and block and bee.
 C   G₇   C   G₇
B is for baby waving at me.
 C   F   C
C is for crayons, car, and cat.
G₇   C   G₇   C
C is for clown in a funny striped hat.

Jean Warren

I Found a Letter

Sung to: *Skip to My Lou*

F
I found an *A*, how about you?
G
I found an *A*, how about you?
F
I found an *A*, how about you?
G   F
I found an *A*, and you can, too.

Substitute the name of any letter for *A*.

Elizabeth McKinnon

We Found a Letter

Sung to: *The Farmer in the Dell*

        D
We found a *B* today.

We found a *B* today.

B, *B*, we found a *B*.
      A₇   D
We found a *B* today!

Substitute the name of any letter for *B*.

Gayle Bittinger

Opposites
Sung to: *Twinkle, Twinkle, Little Star*

    C   F   C
The opposite of left is right.
    G_7 C G_7 C
The opposite of day is night.
C G_7 C G_7
Now we come to short and long.
C G_7 C G_7
After that, right and wrong.
C   F   C
Lost and found, sick and well.
G_7 C G_7 C
How many opposites can you tell?

C   F   C
Heavy and light are not the same.
G_7 C G_7 C
Don't you like our opposite game?
C G_7 C G_7
Next, I think of stop and go.
C G_7 C G_7
After that, high and low.
C   F   C
First and last, fast and slow.
G_7 C G_7 C
How many opposites do you know?

Mildred Hoffman
Tacoma, WA

Do You Know Your Opposites?
Sung to: *Did You Ever See a Lassie?*

F
Do you know your opposites,
      C_7 F
Your opposites, your opposites?

Do you know your opposites?
      C_7 F
Then sing some with me.
    C_7 F
There's up and down,
    C_7 F
There's lost and found.

Do you know your opposites?
     C_7 F
Then sing some with me.

F
Do you know your opposites,
     C_7 F
Your opposites, your opposites?

Do you know your opposites?
     C_7 F
Then sing some with me.
    C_7 F
There's in and out,
    C_7 F
There's whisper and shout.

Do you know your opposites?
     C_7 F
Then sing some with me.

Additional verses: There's hot and cold, there's young and old; There's fast and slow, there's stop and go; There's day and night, there's left and right.

Janice Bodenstedt
Jackson, MI

Up and Down
Sung to: *Here We Go Looby Loo*

D
See us reach up, up, up.

              A₇
See us reach down, down, down.

D
See us reach up, up, up.

A₇   D
Now see us twirl all around.

Elizabeth McKinnon

Hard and Soft
Sung to: *London Bridge*

C
Touch the rock, it feels so hard,

G₇   C
Feels so hard, feels so hard.

Touch the rock, it feels so hard.

G₇   C
Hard, hard, rock.

C
Touch the fur, it feels so soft,

G₇   C
Feels so soft, feels so soft.

Touch the fur, it feels so soft.

G₇   C
Soft, soft, fur.

Repeat, substituting the names of other hard and soft things for *rock* and *fur*.

Elizabeth McKinnon

Quiet and Noisy
Sung to: *Row, Row, Row Your Boat*

C
Let's sing a quiet song,

Let's whisper it today.

Let's make our voices, oh, so soft
G   C
As we sing today.

C
Let's sing a noisy song,

Let's shout it out this way.

Let's make our voices, oh, so loud
G   C
As we sing today!

Elizabeth McKinnon

It Opens and Closes
Sung to: *Did You Ever See a Lassie?*

    F
Have you ever seen a door,
 C₇   F
A door, a door?

Have you ever seen a door
    C₇   F
That works like this?
 C₇   F
It opens and closes,
 C₇   F
It opens and closes.
       F
Have you ever seen a door
   C₇   F
That works like this?

Repeat, each time substituting the name of a different item that opens and closes for *door*.

Elizabeth McKinnon

Empty and Full
Sung to: *Row, Row, Row Your Boat*

C
Fill, fill, fill the bag.

Fill it now with me.

First it's empty, then it's full,
G   C
Full as full can be.

Elizabeth McKinnon

Right Hand, Left Hand
Sung to: *Mary Had a Little Lamb*

C
My right hand touches my right foot,
   (Touch right hand to body parts named.)
G₇   C
My right knee, my right eye.

My right hand touches my right ear.
G₇   C
All on my right side.

C
My left hand touches my left foot,
   (Touch left hand to body parts named.)
G₇   C
My left knee, my left eye.

My left hand touches my left ear.
G₇   C
All on my left side.

Laura Egge
Lake Oswego, OR

Clock Song
Sung to: *Hickory, Dickory, Dock*

C   G₇   C
Hickory, dickory, dock.

         G₇   C
The time is one o'clock.

See the little hand
F
Point to one.
C   G₇   C
Hickory, dickory, dock.

C   G₇   C
Hickory, dickory, dock.

         G₇   C
The time is two o'clock.

See the little hand
F
Point to two.
C   G₇   C
Hickory, dickory, dock.

C   G₇   C
Hickory, dickory, dock.

         G₇   C
The time is three o'clock.

See the little hand
F
Point to three.
C   G₇   C
Hickory, dickory, dock.

As you continue with similar verses, naming hours up to 12 o'clock, hold up a play clock and move the hands to the appropriate times.

Elizabeth McKinnon

The Clock Goes Round Each Day
Sung to: *Row, Row, Row Your Boat*

C
Tick, tock, tick-tock-tick.

The clock goes round each day.

It tells us when it's time to work
        G   C
And when it's time to play.

Adapted Traditional

My Little Watch
Sung to: *Twinkle, Twinkle, Little Star*

C   F   C
See my little watch right here?
(Form circle with thumb and finger.)

G₇   C   G₇   C
Hold it closely to your ear.
(Hold circle up to ear.)

C   G₇   C   G₇
Hear it ticking, ticking fast.
C   G₇   C   G₇
It tells us when our playtime's past.
C   F   C
See my little watch right here.
(Form circle with thumb and finger.)

G₇   C   G₇   C
Hold it closely to your ear.
(Hold circle up to ear.)

Repeat, each time substituting a different word, such as *storytime* or *snacktime*, for *playtime*.

Adapted Traditional

Days of the Week

Sung to: *Yankee Doodle*

C   G₇
Sunday, Monday, Tuesday, Wednesday,
C   G₇
Thursday, Friday, Saturday.
C   F
Don't ask me not to sing it again,
       G₇   C
Because I'll do it anyway!
F
Sunday, Monday, Tuesday, Wednesday,
C
Thursday, Friday, Saturday.
F
Sunday, Monday, Tuesday, Wednesday,
C   G₇   C
Thursday, Friday, Saturday.

Laura Egge
Lake Oswego, OR

Days

Sung to: *Frere Jacques*

C
Sunday, Monday, Tuesday, Wednesday,

And Thursday and Friday.

Don't forget the last day,

Don't forget the last day,

Saturday. Let's all play!

Deborah A. Roessel
Flemington, NJ

Count the Days

Sung to: *Twinkle, Twinkle, Little Star*

C   F   C
Come along and count with me.
G₇   C   G₇   C
There are seven days, you see.
C   G₇   C   G₇
Sunday, Monday, Tuesday, too,
C   G₇   C   G₇
Wednesday, Thursday, just for you.
C   F   C
Friday, Saturday, that's the end.
G₇   C   G₇   C
Now let's sing our song again!

Judy Hall
Wytheville, VA

Oh, If You Know the Month

Sung to: *If You're Happy and You Know It*

     F   C
Oh, if you know the month, shout it out.
   (January!)
     C   F
Oh, if you know the month, shout it out.
   (January!)
     Bb
Oh, if you know the month,
     F
Oh, if you know the month,
     C   F
Oh, if you know the month, shout it out.
   (January!)

     F   C
Oh, if you know the day, whisper it now.
   (Monday.)
     C   F
Oh, if you know the day, whisper it now.
   (Monday.)
     Bb
Oh, if you know the day,
     F
Oh, if you know the day,
     C   F
Oh, if you know the day, whisper it now.
   (Monday.)

     F   C
Oh, if you know the date, shout it out.
   (The first!)
     C   F
Oh, if you know the date, shout it out.
   (The first!)
     Bb
Oh, if you know the date,
     F
Oh, if you know the date,
     C   F
Oh, if you know the date, shout it out.
   (The first!)

Substitute the names of the present month, day, and date for *January, Monday,* and *the first.*

Sharon K. Engel
Oshkosh, WI

Months of the Year

Sung to: *Skip to My Lou*

F
Come and sing along with me,
C7
Come and sing along with me,
F
Come and sing along with me
     C7   F
The twelve months of the year.

F
January, February, March, and April,
C7
May, June, July, and August,
F
September, October, November, and December
C7   F
Are the twelve months of the year.

Karen M. Smith
Bluemont, VA

Weather
Sung to: *Frere Jacques*

C
What's the weather, what's the weather?

Do you know, do you know?

Do you see the sun out?

Is there rain all about?

Is there snow, is there snow?

Gayle Bittinger

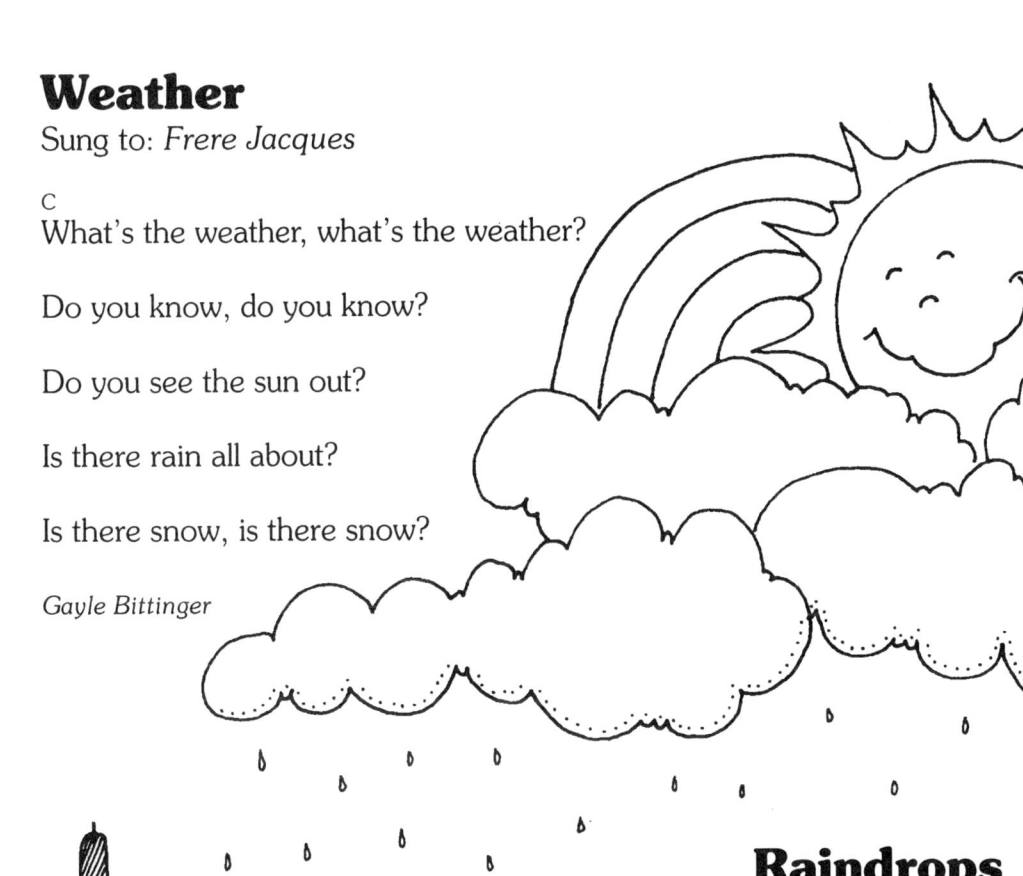

Raindrops
Sung to: *Frere Jacques*

C
Raindrops falling, raindrops falling

From the sky, from the sky.

Put up an umbrella,

Put up an umbrella

Nice and dry, nice and dry!

C
Shower's over, shower's over.

Sun's aglow, sun's aglow.

See the pretty flowers,

See the pretty flowers

In a row, in a row.

Jean Warren

Golden Sunlight
Sung to: *I'm a Little Teapot*

C   F   C
Oh, the big round sun, it shines so bright,
G₇   C   G₇   C
Helps plants grow and gives us light.
              F   C
When the golden sunlight shines on me,
          G₇   C
I'm warm and happy as can be!

Susan Hodges

Weather **7**

Wind, Wind
Sung to: *Row, Row, Row Your Boat*

C
Wind, wind, blow and blow

Gently through the trees.

Blow and blow and blow and blow.
G   C
Make a little breeze.

C
Wind, wind, blow the clouds,

Blow them through the sky.

Blow and blow and blow and blow.
G   C
Make the clouds roll by.

Diane Thom
Maple Valley, WA

Snowflakes Falling
Sung to: *Sailing, Sailing*

F
Snowflakes, snowflakes
Bb   F
Falling to the ground.
Bb   F
Each one rests so gently
 Bb   C
And never makes a sound.
F
Snowflakes, snowflakes
Bb   F
Are so pure and white.
 Bb   F
The special thing about them is—
 Bb   C F
No two are alike!

Angela Wolfe-Batten
Dayton, OH

Frost
Sung to: *The Farmer in the Dell*

        D
The frost is on the roof.
   (Point upward.)

The frost is on the ground.
   (Point downward.)

The frost is on the window.
   (Form a window with hands.)
        A7   D
The frost is all around.
   (Gesture right, then left.)

        D
The frost is very icy.
   (Shiver.)

The frost is very bright.
   (Cover eyes with hands.)

The frost is very slippery.
   (Slide one hand over the other.)
        A7   D
The frost is very white!

Lois E. Putnam
Pilot Mountain, NC

76 Weather

The Four Seasons

Sung to: *The Farmer in the Dell*

   D
Oh, autumn time is here.

Oh, autumn time is here.

It's time to watch the leaves fall down.
  A₇   D
Oh, autumn time is here.

   D
Oh, wintertime is here.

Oh, wintertime is here.

It's time to build a snowy fort.
  A₇   D
Oh, wintertime is here.

   D
Oh, springtime is here.

Oh, springtime is here.

It's time to watch the flowers bloom.
  A₇   D
Oh, springtime is here.

   D
Oh, summertime is here.

Oh, summertime is here.

It's time to run and play outside.
  A₇   D
Oh, summertime is here.

Judith Taylor Burtchet
El Dorado, KS

I Like Fall

Sung to: *Skip to My Lou*

  F
Picking apples off the trees,
  C₇
Jumping in a pile of leaves,
  F
Picking pumpkins off the vine—
  C₇   F
I think I like fall just fine!

Diane Thom
Maple Valley, WA

In Wintertime

Sung to: *She'll Be Coming Round the Mountain*

        F
Oh, it blows and, oh, it snows in wintertime!
                                C₇
Oh, it blows and, oh, it snows in wintertime!
        F
Oh, it blows and, oh, it snows,
        B♭
Oh, it blows and, oh, it snows!
        F   C₇   F
Oh, it blows and, oh, it snows in wintertime!

Betty Silkunas
Lansdale, PA

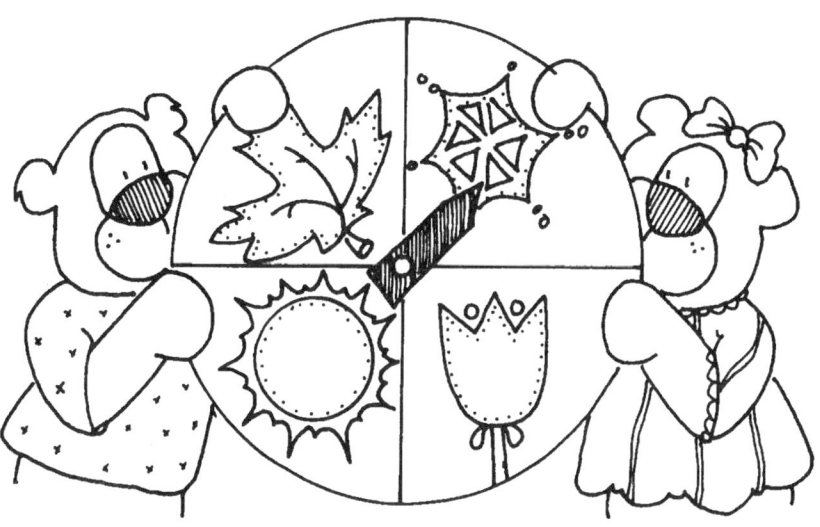

Seasons **77**

Spring Song
Sung to: *Sing a Song of Sixpence*

G
Sing a song of springtime,
D
Sunshine fills the sky.

See the little bluebirds
G
As they fly on by.

Look at all the flowers
C
Blooming pink and blue.
D
What a pretty time to sit
                      G
And watch things start anew!

Kathleen Cubley

Summer's Here
Sung to: *Frere Jacques*

C
Days are longer, sunshine's stronger.

Summer's here, summer's here!

Let's run through the sprinkler.

Let's make lemonade.

Summer's here, summer's here!

Diane Thom
Maple Valley, WA

Oh, Do You Know?

Sung to: *The Muffin Man*

   G
Oh, do you know what color this is,
    (Adult sings while pointing to a color.)
   C   D₇
What color this is, what color this is?
   G
Oh, do you know what color this is?
 D₇   G
Please tell me, if you know.
    (Children respond.)

Substitute a different word, such as *shape, number, letter,* or *animal,* for *color.*

Laura Egge
Lake Oswego, OR

Did You Ever See It?

Sung to: *Did You Ever See a Lassie?*

   F
Did you ever see a shape,
    (Adult sings while pointing to a shape.)
 C₇   F
A shape, a shape?

Did you ever see a shape
 C₇   F
Like this one before?
 C₇   F
The shape is a _____.
    (Everyone sings.)
 C₇   F
The shape is a _____.

Oh yes, we've seen a shape
 C₇   F
Like that one before.

Substitute a different word, such as *color, number, letter,* or *animal,* for *shape.*

Laura Egge
Lake Oswego, OR

What Is It?

Sung to: *Jimmy Crack Corn*

 F   C₇
What is the number I have here?
    (Adult sings while pointing to a number.)
              F
_____ is the number you have there.
    (Children respond.)
            Bb
You knew the answer to that one,
    (Adult sings.)
 C₇   F
So now I'll ask one more.

Substitute a different word, such as *color, shape, letter,* or *animal,* for *number.* For the final verse of the song, end with *So now I'll ask no more.*

Laura Egge
Lake Oswego, OR

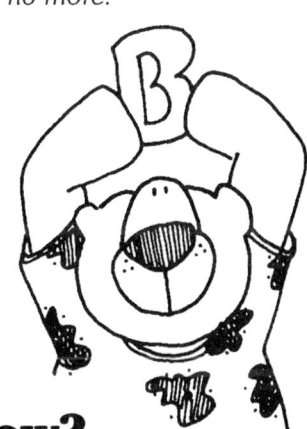

Do You Know?

Sung to: *The Mulberry Bush*

D
Children, children, do you know,
    (Adult sings while holding up a letter.)
A₇
Do you know, do you know,
D
Children, children, do you know
 A₇   D
The letter I'm holding up?
    (Children name letter.)

Substitute a different word, such as *color, shape, number,* or *animal,* for *letter.*

Laura Egge
Lake Oswego, OR

Multiple Concepts

Instant Hands-on Ideas!

FREE sample newsletters available!

Totline® Newsletter and **Super Snack News** are perfect for working with young children because they are put together by the publisher of Totline® Books, a leader in early childhood resources for parents and teachers. Totline books and newsletters are guaranteed to be appropriate, enriching, and fun. Help your children feel good about themselves and their ability to learn by using the hands-on approach to active learning found in these two newsletters!

...en Publishing House
...250, Dept. Z, Everett, WA 98203

Totline® Newsletter

This newsletter offers creative hands-on activities that are designed to be challenging for children ages 2 to 6, yet easy for teachers and parents to do. Minimal preparation time is needed to make maximum use of common, inexpensive materials. Each bimonthly issue includes • seasonal fun • learning games • open-ended art • music and movement • language activities • science fun • reproducible teaching aids • reproducible parent-flyer pages and • Good Earth (environmental awareness) activities. *Totline Newsletter* is perfect for use with an antibias curriculum or to emphasize antibias values in a home environment.

Super Snack News

This newsletter is designed to be reproduced!

With each subscription you are permitted to make up to 200 copies per issue! They make great handouts to parents. Inside this monthly, four-page newsletter are healthy recipes and nutrition tips, plus related songs and activities for young children. Also provided are category guidelines for the CACFP reimbursement program. Sharing *Super Snack News* is a wonderful way to help promote quality childcare.

To receive your FREE copy of either Totline Newsletter or Super Snack News, call 1-800-773-7240.